YOUNG ADULT ELI READERS B1

The **ELI Readers** collection is a complete range of books and plays for readers of all ages, ranging from captivating contemporary stories to timeless classics. There are four series, each catering for a different age group: **First ELI Readers**, **Young ELI Readers**, **Teen ELI Readers** and **Young Adult ELI Readers**. The books are carefully edited and beautifully illustrated to capture the essence of the stories and plots. The readers are supplemented with 'Focus on' texts packed with background cultural information about the writers and their lives and times.

CHANGING THE WORLD!
CHIARA MICHELON

YOUNG ADULT ELI READERS

Chiara Michelon
Changing the World!

English version
Pauline Russo

YOUNG ADULT ELI READERS
Series Editors
Paola Accattoli, Grazia Ancillani, Daniele Garbuglia (Art Director)

Graphic Design
Andersen the Premedia Company

Layout
Emilia Coari

Production Manager
Francesco Capitano

Photo Credits
Shutterstock, Alamy

© 2023 ELI S.r.l.
P.O. Box 6 - 62019 Recanati - Italia
Tel. +39 071 750701
Fax +39 071 977851
support@elipublishing.com
www.elipublishing.com

Typeset in 11,5 / 15pt Monotype Dante

ERA 344.10
ISBN 978-88-536-3970-7

www.eligradedreaders.com

Printed in Italy by Tecnostampa
Pigini Group Printing Division – Loreto – Trevi

Disclaimer
This book has been written using information in the public domain from official sites, online biographies and interviews, with the sole reason to provide useful information from reliable sources, known to be true about persons of great ethical and social importance. It is not intended as a complete biography of the individuals described here, but as a simple introduction to further study. Although every care has been taken to ensure the accuracy of the information in this publication, we apologise for any inaccuracies there may be and if we have missed something, we would ask you to write to us at: redazione@elionline.com

Contents

6	Pre-reading Activities
8	**Malala Yousafzai**
14	Activities
16	**Nelson Mandela**
22	Activities
24	**Wangari Maathai**
30	Activities
32	**Muhammad Yunus**
38	Activities
40	**Rigoberta Menchú Tum**
46	Activities
48	**Thich Nhat Hanh**
54	Activities
56	**Leymah Gbowee**
62	Activities
64	**Kailash Satyarthi**
70	Activities
72	**Maria Ressa**
78	Activities
80	**Ian Kiernan**
86	Activities
88	**Dossier – Let's not forget**
90	**Dossier – Peacekeeping Organisations**
92	**Dossier – Important words**
94	Test Yourself
96	Syllabus

The parts of the text on the audio are indicated by the following symbols: **Start** ▶ **End** ■

PRE-READING ACTIVITIES

Writing

1 Do you wish for world peace? Write an email to your friend talking about how you dream of having peace in the world.

Speaking

2 Do you know these famous people? What do you know about them? Tell the class about them.

The 2030 Agenda – Goal 16

3 Have you heard of "Extinction Rebellion"? What do you think it is? Discuss in pairs and compare your ideas with the rest of the class. You can look for information on the internet.

Where are they from?

4 Match the photos of the following famous people to their country of origin.

1 ☐ Malala Yousafzai

5 ☐ Rigoberta Menchú Tum

2 ☐ Nelson Mandela

6 ☐ Thich Nhat Hanh

3 ☐ Wangari Maathai

7 ☐ Leyman Gbowee

4 ☐ Muhammad Yunus

8 ☐ Kailash Satyarthi

a Bangladesh
b Vietnam
c South Africa
d Liberia
e India
f Kenya
g Pakistan
h Guatemala

THE RIGHT* TO AN EDUCATION

Malala Yousafzai

A secret blog

▶ 2 Malala was born on 12th July 1997 in the Swat valley in Pakistan, in a peaceful village called Mingora. The Yousafzai family, who were Pashtuns, were educated people. Malala's grandparents were teachers and her father was a human rights activist*. Her parents named Malala, their first child, after a famous Pakistan heroine. In her country, male children are preferred but her parents welcomed her with great happiness. Malala was very intelligent and worked hard at school. She wanted to be independent and have a good job when she grew up.

At the end of 2007, the Taliban invaded the region where the Yousafzai lived and they had to go and live with relatives in Haripur. No entertainment was allowed, and women did not even have the right to do simple things like going to school, and were forced to wear the burqa*, something that Malala thought was really unfair. She worked in secret for the BBC, writing a blog about life in Pakistan and the things that women and children were not allowed to do. She wrote the blog under the name Gul Makai, "cornflower". She also made two documentaries with the New York Times, one on

> " I don't mind if I have to sit on the floor at school. All I want is education. And I'm afraid of no one."

right: what a person is allowed to have or do, and not have it taken away
activist: a person who works hard to make important changes in society
burqa: a dark veil worn by Muslim women which covers their face but not their eyes

THE RIGHT TO AN EDUCATION

the schools closing and another on the problems of girl students.

Everyone knew that Malala had written the Gul Makai blog. In December 2011, the Pakistan government gave her the National Peace Prize. At that time, the Taliban were losing control of the country and it seemed that life was returning to normal. She returned to Mingora, and more importantly, she was able to go back to school, even if she still had to wear the burqa. Malala was happy because she had missed going to school a lot.

The assassination attempt

On 9th October 2012, near exam times, Malala was on a bus with her schoolfriends, when two Talibans stopped the bus and asked where Malala was. When they saw her, they shot at her and hit her in the head. She was taken to hospital, first in Pashawar and then to Birmingham in Great Britain. Fortunately, she did not die. The Taleban had wanted to eliminate her just because she had become a symbol of the fight for the right to an education. Thousands of children from all over the world wrote to her in hospital. While she was there, she continued to read and study, and she realised that, sadly, she would have to make a new life for herself, far from her home country.

Her family could not return to their country because the Taliban had taken control of Pakistan again. However, thanks to the media attention around her attack, the United Nations

Women in Pakistan

Still today, in Pakistan, women suffer discrimination*. Almost all women are not allowed to work, study or are not even free to leave their own homes. Some have to marry men who are much older than they are, even if they don't love them. Women are considered less important than men. The birth of a baby girl is a problem for families and is not a happy event.

discrimination looking at people differently because of age, race or gender

Malala
Yousafzai

started a petition* demanding that, by 2015, all children should be allowed to go to school. This was the first official document in Pakistan on the right to education. While Malala was living in Britain, the Pakistan President, Zardari, gave 10 million dollars to education and the Malala Foundation was also started to help girls all over the world to get an education.

The right to an education

On the day of her sixteenth birthday, Malala was invited to make a speech at the United Nations building in New York. In front of a very important audience, she spoke about her fight for the right to education and invited everyone to fight, in any way possible, for the right of every child, not just girls, to have an education. Education

Schoolgirls in Pakistan.

is, in fact, the only way to fight discrimination. For the occasion, she wore the shawl* that had belonged to Benazir Bhutto, the political leader who had tried to change Pakistan.

In 2014, she became the youngest person to win the Nobel Peace Prize, which she shared with the Indian activist, Kailash Satyarthi, for their fight for all children to have an education. *"Let us pick up our books and our pens, they are the most powerful weapons. One child, one teacher, one book, one pen can change the world."* Many schools

> " *Education is power for women. The Talibans are closing girls' schools because they don't want women to have power.* "

petition a document signed by many people to protest about something
shawl a piece of cloth you wear on your shoulders

THE RIGHT TO AN **EDUCATION**

The 2030 Agenda

The 2030 Agenda is a programme of action for all people, the planet and well-being. It was signed on 25th September 2015 by the 193 member countries of the United Nations and has 17 goals for sustainable development. These should be achieved by 2030 and are environmental*, economical and social in nature. The programme is not the answer to all world problems but is a good common base to start from and go towards building a different world that allows everyone to live in a sustainable way.

today remember her role as a female activist, especially on 20th November, when they celebrate World Children's Day. Her work is based on ideas, but also on doing real things, like opening schools for people escaping from dangerous situations in their own countries.

> " *When the whole world is silent, even one voice becomes powerful.* "

She became one of the heroes of Global Goals, or the 2030 Agenda, together with many other activists and celebrities like Anastacia, Kate Winslet, Jennifer Lopez and Bill Gates. In 2015, world leaders promised, within fifteen years, to complete 17 goals towards sustainable* development. The most important goals include stopping extreme poverty, fighting against inequality* and injustice*, and stopping climate change*. Together with her friend, Greta Thunberg, Malala has said that the climate crisis is having negative effects on basic human rights, like the right to education.

environmental regarding the environment, the natural world we live in
sustainable helping the environment
inequality not seen as the same as others, not being equal
injustice something that is not right or fair
climate change when weather patterns become different because of pollution

No fear

Malala studied philosophy, politics and economics at Oxford University, so that she could become a politician and help give the women in her own country a future. She got her university degree in 2020 and then took some time during the pandemic to try and understand what she wanted to do with her life, like anyone of her age. In 2021, she married Asser Malik, in Birmingham, in an Islamic ceremony in the Urdu language.

Malala continues her fight for civil rights, education and women's rights. She does this with great courage and without any fear, telling the truth and as an international symbol for the women who are fighting for their right to education and freedom.

I am Malala

This book tells the story of Malala's life. She wrote it together with Christina Lamb, an international journalist and expert on Pakistan and Afghanistan. It is a very emotional story about her courage and her dream to change the world. *"You must speak the truth. The truth will abolish fear".*

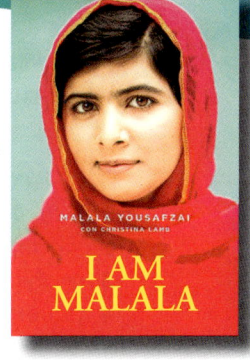

ACTIVITIES

Reading Comprehension

1 **Choose the correct answer.**

1 Malala is the name of:
   a ☐ a teacher in Pakistan
   b ☐ a heroine from Pakistan
   c ☐ Malala's grandmother

2 The burqa is:
   a ☐ a dark veil
   b ☐ a Taliban book
   c ☐ something prohibited by Muslims

3 Where was Malala attacked?
   a ☐ At school
   b ☐ On a bus
   c ☐ In front of her house

4 Which country did Malala have to live in?
   a ☐ Afghanistan
   b ☐ Italy
   c ☐ Great Britain

5 In which city is the headquarters of the United Nations?
   a ☐ London
   b ☐ New York
   c ☐ Paris

6 How many goals does the 2030 Agenda have?
   a ☐ 20   **b** ☐ 15   **c** ☐ 17

2a **Work with a partner. Discuss what the following words mean to you. Write a short definition of them and compare them with the class.**

1 education: ....
2 inequality: ....
3 prohibited: ....
4 poverty: ....

2b Now think about the opposite meaning of these words. Write a short definition of them and compare them with the class.

1 education: the opposite is ....
2 inequality: the opposite is ....
3 prohibited: the opposite is ....
4 poverty: the opposite is ....

Writing

3 Imagine you are Malala. How would you start your autobiography? Start with "I am Malala."

I am Malala...

Roleplay

4 Work in pairs. Decide who will play the role of Malala and who will be the journalist. Write 5 questions and answers for a TV interview. You could also make a video of the interview with your mobile phone to show to your class.

HUMAN RIGHTS

Nelson Mandela

From a tribe* to politics

▶ 3 Nelson Mandela was born 18th July 1918 into the Thembu royal family, a tribe of the Xhosa people from South Africa. His father was the head of the tribe and he grew up listening to stories about his ancestors* and their fight for freedom. He too dreamed of helping his people in their fight to be free. While he was studying law in Fort Hare, his great desire* for justice grew and when he organised demonstrations* with Oliver Tambo, his university told him to leave. He found a job as a guard* at the Crown Mines in Johannesburg and it was then that politics started to become an important part of his life. He decided not to become head of his tribe and he didn't marry the woman that the village leaders had chosen for him, which was against his family traditions.

Mandela knew very well that it was education that would make him a good politician who would respect the rights of every person, especially the weakest. *"Education is the most powerful weapon which you can use to change the world"*. In 1944, together with Oliver and Walter Sisulu, he formed the Youth League of the African National Congress, because he saw that his people were suffering and that the laws were becoming even more unjust and impossible to accept. This organisation fought for black South Africans to have the same rights as white people. After finishing his studies at a different university, he opened the first lawyer's office for

tribe group of people of same race
ancestors family members born many years ago
desire something you really want a lot
demonstration crowds coming together to show they are against something
guard a person who protects people or things

HUMAN RIGHTS

black people, the poor and social outcasts*. During these years he helped to organise marches and non-violent demonstrations against discrimination. When Mandela was a young man, black people in South Africa had very few rights. They were not allowed to vote, become politicians or even buy land. Those were difficult years for non white people. In 1948, laws were passed to separate whites from blacks and so, apartheid began.

> " There is no easy road to freedom!! "

Apartheid

The word apartheid means "separation". This was the word used to describe the policy of race discrimination decided by the white government in South Africa after the Second World War. Since the times of the first colonies in South Africa, less than 9% of the population was white, but the white people were more powerful. Whites and blacks had to live in separate areas. They weren't allowed to marry, sit at the same table, take the same bus, or go to the same schools. Apartheid was finally officially abolished* in 1993 by the members of the United Nations.

The first black president

Mandela loved that Gandhi's demonstrations were peaceful because he believed that non-violence was the only possible way to solve the problems in his country. During his long life, he was sent to prison many times, the first time being in 1956. At the age of 46 he was sent to prison for life after a trial in Rivonia. He stayed in prison till 1990 and during these 27 years in prison he had no contact with the outside world. In this period he became

---

outcast someone who is not wanted by others in society

abolished eliminated, ended

Nelson Mandela

ill with tuberculosis but refused help from anyone. He believed that he was in prison unjustly and would never change his mind. In prison he studied a lot and exercised for an hour every day. He thought that sport could change the world because it brings people together. It speaks to young people in a language that they can understand and brings hope where there is very little. In sport there are no blacks or whites. There are only human beings who want to win.

When he became president, he used sport, especially rugby, as a way of uniting men and women and a way of rebuilding his country. Rugby is a sport with important human values. In the Rugby World Cup in South Africa, Mandela used rugby, a sport usually played by white people, to bring his country together and make South Africans proud of their nationality.

He was the most famous political prisoner in the world and there were demonstrations all over the world in his name. In the meantime, little by little, things were changing in South Africa. For example, black students were allowed to go to universities for white people. Mandela understood that the only way to a better future in his country was to have a good and non-violent relationship between blacks and whites. Shortly after leaving prison on 11th February 1990,

" *I have cherished the ideal of a democratic and free society in which all persons live together in harmony* and with equal opportunities. It is an ideal which I hope to live for and to achieve. But if needs be, it is an ideal for which I am prepared to die."* .

harmony living well together

Rosa Parks

The story of Rosa Parks is a perfect example of how a simple action can change lives. In Alabama on 1st December 1955, Rosa was returning home from work by bus. She sat in the first row of the area where both blacks or whites could sit, but where a black person would have to give their seat to a white person. When the driver asked her a few minutes later to get up, Rosa refused. She said, *"I wasn't physically tired, I was just tired of giving in*"*. This one small action changed history and led the world to justice and freedom.

thanks also to the South African President Klerk, his great popularity led him to becoming the first black President of South Africa.

His government was the first one to include different races and Mandela's goal was to bring South Africa together in peace, to unite* white and black people. These were years of great change in his country. As President, he investigated crimes against human rights during apartheid and promoted peace in the different communities. He also signed a new democratic constitution* in 1997.

giving in surrendering, accepting what others want
unite to bring or come together

democratic constitution a law which makes all people equal

Nelson Mandela

A legend

In 1999, Mandela retired from public life but continued with his humanitarian work and his fight for peace and human understanding, especially outside South Africa. The Nelson Mandela Foundation was started to make the world, not just South Africa, a better place to live in, by helping those suffering from discrimination and poverty, and fighting for their rights to freedom, education and health.

> *" Your freedom and mine cannot be separated. Freedom is indivisible "*

He is probably the politician who has received the most awards* in the world. As well as the Nobel Peace Prize in 1993, he received 250 other prizes! Mandela fought all of his life for black people's rights and became a legend who was famous all around the world for his fight for social justice.

In 2009, the United Nations declared that his birthday, 18th July, would be celebrated as Nelson Mandela International Day, to promote* justice, peace and unity all over the world.

He died at his home in Johannesburg on 5th December 2013.

award prize, something you win for doing something good
promote to make important, encourage

ACTIVITIES

Grammar

1 **Complete the sentences with the correct time expression from the list below.**

> today • from that moment • in the year • when • while • that day • after • at that time

We are _____ (1) 1955. Rosa Parks is returning home by bus, _____ (2) working all day. _____ (3) she is looking for a place to sit, she sees that there is only one free seat, near the special area where both whites and blacks can sit. _____ (4) she sits down, the driver comes and asks her to get up. Rosa doesn't get up. "_____ (5) I wasn't physically tired, I was just tired of giving in". This one small action changed history and _____ (6) the world fought for justice and freedom. _____ (7) apartheid is just a bad memory, but _____ (8) it was a sad reality.

Writing

2 **Answer the questions.**

1 In what way did Nelson Mandela not follow his family traditions?
....
....

2 What is *apartheid*?
....
....

3 Why did Mandela believe that sport could change the world?
....
....

4 What is celebrated on 18th July and why?
....
....

Think On!

The 2030 Agenda - Goal 10

3 **Goal 10 of the 2030 Agenda is *"Reduced Inequalities"*.**
One of its targets 10.2 is: *"empower and promote the social, economic and political inclusion of all, irrespective of age, sex, disability, race, ethnicity, origin, religion or economic or other status"*. Target 10.3 is: *"Ensure equal opportunity and reduce inequalities of outcome, including eliminating discriminatory laws, policies and practices"*. In other words, making sure that all people of all ages, gender, race, religion and social status are treated the same and with no discrimination.
What do you think about these ideas? Do you think it is talking about racism? What could be done to reach these goals?

....
....
....
....
....
....

Vocabulary

4 **Choose a word from the box below and write it next to the correct definition.**

abolished • ancestors • demonstration • desire • outcast • unite

1 ....: someone who is not wanted by others in society
2 ....: something you really want a lot
3 ....: to bring or come together
4 ....: eliminated; ended
5 ....: crowds coming together to protest against something
6 ....: family members born many years before in the past

PROTECTING THE ENVIRONMENT

Wangari Maathai

The Tree Woman

▶ 4 Wangari Maathai was born in 1940 in central Kenya when her country was still a British colony. At that time the female children of *kikuyu* farmers didn't go to school, but her brother persuaded their mother to send his little sister to the village school. She was intelligent and interested in everything, so a teacher moved her to a primary school in Nyeri, where lessons were not in her tribe's language, but in English. She quickly learned the new language and got excellent results in all her subjects. She became a Catholic and then went to the only girls' high school in Kenya, at Limuru, near Nairobi.

Kikuyu

The kikuyu is the largest ethnic group of people in Kenya. They speak a language called kikuyu and are farmers who live in the central mountain areas between Nairobi and Mount Kenya. After the country got its independence in 1963, it became part of the Kenyan nation. The first famous kikuyu politician, Jomo Kenyatta, was the first president of the new state.

After finishing high school, she was one of 300 African students chosen by the American government to study in the United States, where she received a college scholarship*.

scholarship money given to students to study at university

PROTECTING THE ENVIRONMENT

During this time, she worked in a laboratory, but didn't have enough money to return to Kenya. She took part in African American civil rights demonstrations and environmental protests. When Kenya got its independence* from the United Kingdom, she was studying at the University of Pittsburgh. She became the first Central African woman to get a degree* in biological sciences. In 1966, after almost six years in the United States, she decided to return to Kenya, and she never left it again.

She found work as an assistant in the veterinary* department at the University of Nairobi, where she continued to study and, in 1971, became the first woman to receive a PhD*. She began teaching veterinary science at the University of Nairobi and became president of the National Council of Women of Kenya. As a scientist and environmentalist, she was an example for many women.

Now is the time

While working all around Kenya, she saw with her own eyes the serious damage to the environment and population because of the natural vegetation being destroyed to grow tea and coffee plants. She met with the women from the area, who were suffering because the land was too poor to grow anything. There was no wood for fires and no fields where animals could eat grass. Also, there was no clean water to drink because the rivers were dry.

When she returned home, she saw that the lakes near her village were also starting to become dry and that the streams were no longer there. This was the moment when she decided that something had to be done to stop the deforestation* and protect the environment. Then she had a very clever idea. Let's plant trees. And so began the story of the woman we now know as *"the Tree Woman"*.

independence being free from others to do what you want
degree what you get when you finish studying at university
veterinary type of medicine studied to care for animals
phD (= doctorate) an advanced university course after a degree
deforestation taking away woods and forests

Wangari **Maathai**

> " *The future of the planet concerns all of us, and all of us should do what we can to protect it. As I told the foresters, and the women, you don't need a diploma to plant a tree.* "

The Green Belt*

With the help of the other women in the villages, she collected seeds from the forest, planted them, watered them and cared for them, until the plants were thirty centimetres high. There were indigenous* trees, small plants and fruit trees and the women took great care of them, just like their own children. On World Environment Day, 5th June 1977, they planted 7 trees in a park just outside the Kenyan capital. These trees formed the first *"green belt"*,

green belt area with no buildings, only trees and plants
indigenous living in the place where you were born

Biodiversity

Biodiversity is the marvellous variety of living things on our planet, which act with each other inside particular ecosystems*. However, human actions are causing pollution*, intensive farming*, desertification*, deforestation and climate change, which are all bad for biodiversity. This will cause great damage to the environment, animals and plants. Protecting biodiversity and ecosystems means taking care of air quality, land and water, and not disturbing the seas, oceans, forests, grasslands and other ecosystems

ecosystem biological community of living things
pollution dangerous things in the air or water
intensive farming farming which takes the most out of the land
desertification making land dry and without water

PROTECTING THE ENVIRONMENT

which gave its name to the ecological movement, the *Green Belt Movement*.

Her new and amazing idea was to plant millions of trees, which she managed to do by informing everyone about the problems facing nature and particularly, deforestation. Over 51 million trees were planted in Kenya, more than the population of the country. In the same way that a tree grows from a small seed, this idea grew and gave birth to a great movement which went beyond the borders of Kenya.

The *Green Belt Movement* opened the way to social development, from protecting the environment to fighting discrimination against women and allowing them to work. In fact, Wangari said that the poverty in her country was related to environmental problems and that the solution was to get women involved.

Since 1977, over 30,000 women in Kenya's countryside have grown plants, planted trees, kept beehives* and collected rainwater, all jobs which have earned them money. The *Green Belt Movement* is still working today to create new jobs for women, fight deforestation and protect the biodiversity of the plant and animal life in the world. Wangari became an *"ecofeminist"*.

beehives houses for bees

> "Anybody can dig a hole and plant a tree. But make sure it survives. You have to nurture it, you have to water it, you have to keep at it until it becomes rooted so it can take care of itself."

Wangari
Maathai

The well-being of Africa

After leaving her job at the university, she continued her fight for the environment and became the African symbol of the fight for peace and well-being on the African continent. She worked for the human rights of women and children, in particular, for democracy and a multi-ethnic society. Her work made the whole world aware* of the problems of women, especially African women, whom she helped to fight for a better life.

> *I want to do the right things - I want to plant trees, I want to make sure that the indigenous forests are protected because I know, whatever happens, these are the forests that contain biodiversity, these are the forests that help us retain water when it rains and keep our rivers flowing, these are the forests that many future generations will need.*

Wangari is the first African woman to win the Nobel Peace Prize for *"her contribution to sustainable development, democracy and peace"*. She decided to celebrate this in the way she knew best: by planting a tree in the red earth of the valley of Mount Kenya.

aware notice

ACTIVITIES

Vocabulary

1 Read the clues below and complete the crossword.

1. Look after, defend.
2. To dry up means to take away _____ .
3. The doctor who cares for sick animals.
4. Group of people with same ideals.
5. Born in the place where they live.
6. The language Wangari learned at primary school.
7. Type of farming that takes the most out of the land.
8. These are eliminated with deforestation.
9. The biggest ethnic group in Kenya that Wangari belonged to.
10. Wangari collected and planted these.

Speaking

2 Work in pairs. In this chapter, we read about respect for the environment and women who are fighting to protect our planet. As well as Greta Thunberg, the Swedish activist who is fighting climate change, there is also another young woman, Vanessa Nakate, who introduced "Fridays for Future" in her home country of Uganda. Find out about Vanessa, what she has done and what she believes in, then compare your notes with your classmates. Would you prefer to be like Greta or Vanessa?

Writing The 2030 Agenda - Goal 13

3 We can fight against climate change in many ways and on different levels. Write 10 things you could do to respect the environment and protect biodiversity. For example, " Don't throw plastic into the sea" ...

1 ....
2 ....
3 ....
4 ....
5 ....
6 ....
7 ....
8 ....
9 ....
10 ....

Grammar

4 Put the verbs in brackets into the Simple Past Tense.

At the 20th Olympic Winter Games in Turin in 2006, 8 women **(1)** .... *(carry)* the Olympic flag into the stadium. These women **(2)** .... *(be)* celebrities in their own fields. They **(3)** .... *(come)* from various countries and **(4)** .... *(have)* different backgrounds. As symbols of peace, tolerance and dialogue, they **(5)** .... *(represent)* all women. Who **(6)** .... *(be)* they? The Italian actress and UNHCR ambassador, **Sophia Loren**; Chilean writer **Isabel Allende**; Moroccan athlete **Nawal El Moutawakel**, the first African Muslim woman to win a gold medal; **Susan Sarandon**, American actress and Unicef ambassador; the Italian skier **Manuela Di Centa**, who **(7)** .... *(win)* 7 Olympic medals and **(8)** .... *(be)* the first Italian woman to climb Mt Everest; the athlete **Maria Mutola**, the first woman from Mozambique to win a gold medal; the Cambodian activist, **Somaly Mam**; and **Wangari Maathai**.

THE FIGHT AGAINST POVERTY

Muhammad Yunus

A world without poverty

▶ 5 Muhammad was born in the city of Chittagong, an important business centre in Bangladesh, on 28th June 1940. After getting his economics degree there, he went to Vanderbilt University in Tennessee in the United States of America to study for a Ph.D. He became a professor of economics and stayed in the United States until 1972, when he returned to Bangladesh and became head of the economics department at the university in Chittagong.

In 1974, there were terrible floods in Bangladesh and hundreds of thousands of people died from hunger and suffered extreme poverty. Every morning, when Muhammad was going to the university, he saw many poor people in the streets, asking for money and food, which made him feel uncomfortable. He understood that the economics he was teaching to his students was very different from real life in his own country, where people were living in great poverty. "From that day I decided to forget theory and take lessons in reality. To do this, I didn't have to go far. Reality was all around. I just had to come out of the classroom".

> 66 Here we were talking about economic development, about investing billions of dollars in various programmes, and I could see it wasn't billions of dollars people needed right away. 99

THE FIGHT AGAINST POVERTY

He went into the street, among the people and real life, to study the economics of a rural* village. He took his students to visit houses in the nearby village of Jobra, where they asked the people questions about their difficult living conditions. The workers bought simple materials on credit* and earned very little money, or they borrowed money from money lenders*. He asked his students to make a list of all the people in Jobra who were asking for loans* and to count how much the total was. It was 856 *take*, less than 30 dollars. It wasn't much money, but it was a lot to the poorest families. He discovered that the Bengalese were not poor because they were stupid or lazy, but because the banks in the country did not help them. To make his dream of 'a world without poverty' come true, he had to take action. Professor Yunus used economics in the fight against poverty by inventing something really different in an agricultural country: a modern micro-credit system.

Developing countries

This term refers to change, from an economical point of view but also from the point of view of modernity and social change. These countries often start from low living standards, low incomes* and high levels of poverty, as well as from low levels of industry and low human development. The development of a country is measured on GDP per head, the rate of literacy* and life expectancy*.

rural in the countryside
credit borrowing money which then has to be paid back
money lenders people you borrow money from illegally
loans money you borrow which has to be paid back
income money you earn for working
literacy being able to read and write
life expectancy how long you will live for

Muhammad
Yunus

The banker to the poor

He gave the first loan of 27 American dollars to a group of women from a village near Chittagong, who made furniture and objects from bamboo*. They were having to sell their products to the bamboo sellers, or borrow money from money lenders. They earned very little money and were becoming poorer and poorer. Traditional banks weren't interested in lending money to such small businesses because of low profits* and high risks.

> "One day our grandchildren will go to museums to see what poverty was like."

Professor Yunus and his colleagues went into the poorest areas of Bangladesh, going from village to village, lending a few dollars to anyone who wanted to start a business. He concentrated on women and persuaded them to start *"cooperatives"*, businesses which involved a large number of people from the village. They called him "the banker to the poor".

At a meeting organised by the Central Bank, he presented his plan called *"Financing the poor in rural areas"*. He explained how to organise loans and make it easy for the money to be paid back. It was a good idea but the Governors of the Banks weren't interested. The only one to believe in his idea was the Deputy Governor of the Central Bank.

bamboo wooden canes used to make furniture   **profits** the money you earn from selling something

THE FIGHT AGAINST POVERTY

The village bank

In 1976, Professor Yunus founded* the first bank in the world to give loans to businessmen who were too poor to get credit from traditional banks. It was called the Grameen Bank, or "the village bank" and he was its manager until 2011. He wanted to help his people to have a better standard of life and he thought that being able to get a loan was a basic human right. This bank is really different from other banks because it works on trust and not on interest rates*. Customers don't go to the bank, the bank employees go to the people in the villages, so that poor people don't feel uncomfortable about going to a strange place.

The *"Grameen Method"* goes beyond the idea of micro-credit. Professor Yunus had the idea of increasing the responsibilities and abilities of the borrower. It's the only way that micro-credit can help a person to improve and have an income, a job and independence. All of these things are very positive for the community.

According to Muhammad, every person should be able to have their own business and not have to suffer poverty and usury*. Since it opened, the bank has lent more than 5 billion dollars to more than 5 million customers. Its success has led to it being copied in countries all over the world.

found (infinitive) to start, to build
interest rates a percentage added to loans when paid back
usury lending money illegally to poor people and adding very high interest rates

Muhammad
Yunus

Social business

Professor Yumus continued looking for solutions to poverty and inequality. He developed a new business model called "social business". Social business helps the community, not just the individual businessman, and concentrates on helping society rather than concentrating only on profits. It's about finding a solution to social problems and working for the freedom and well-being of the community.

Micro-credit for women

The micro-credit model called the *"Yunus system"* changed the World Bank's way of thinking and was used in over 20 developing countries. More than 90% of the loans are made to businesses owned by women because they have families to feed and they are able to work better and for longer.

Work on a tea plantation.

Today, Professor Yunus is a member of the UN Foundation's Board of Directors and he has received many international prizes. In 2006 he shared the Nobel Peace Prize with the Grameen Bank. The reason for this award has a very important message: *"for their efforts to create economic and social development from below. Lasting peace can not be achieved unless large population groups find ways in which to break out of poverty. Micro-credit is one such means. Development from below also serves to advance democracy and human rights. Micro-credit has proved to be an important liberating force in societies where women in particular have to struggle"*.

ACTIVITIES

Reading Comprehension

1 **Which sentences are true (T) or false (F)?**

		T	F
1	Muhammad Yunus studied at university in Bangladesh.	☐	☐
2	Yunus graduated but didn't want to teach at the university.	☐	☐
3	There were terrible floods in Bangladesh.	☐	☐
4	There was great economic growth in the country.	☐	☐
5	Money lenders lend money illegally and want higher interest.	☐	☐
6	Professor Yunus went to the villages with his students.	☐	☐
7	He thought the Bengalese were poor because they were stupid.	☐	☐
8	Interest rates are percentages which are added to the cost of loans.	☐	☐
9	The Grameen Bank is also called *"the bank of the poor"*.	☐	☐
10	Micro-credit lends more money to businesses run by men.	☐	☐

2 **Fill in the gaps with the correct number.**

> 5,000,000 • 90% • 1974 • 27 • 1940 • 2011

1 Muhammad Yunus was born in _____ .
2 Bangladesh had floods in the year _____ .
3 The first loan given was _____ American dollars.
4 He was manager of the Grameen Bank until _____.
5 More than _____ of the loans are to women.
6 There are more than _____ micro-credit customers.

Writing

3 Answer the questions.

1 Why is more money given to women's projects?
....

2 What does "*developing countries*" mean?
....

3 Explain the meaning of "*social business*", in your own words.
....

4 When did Yunus decide to leave the university, and why?
....

Vocabulary

4 The word "*fair*" in English has various meanings. Look at the definitions below and, using a dictionary, decide which is the wrong definition.

- ☐ 1 Adjective used to describe good weather.
- ☐ 2 Another way to describe hair or skin that is light, not dark.
- ☐ 3 Payment made to travel by bus or train.
- ☐ 4 Adjective meaning right or just.
- ☐ 5 A place where there are rides like carousels, roller-coasters and other fun things to do.

Think On! Agenda 2030 - Goals 1 and 8

5 Goal 1 (*No Poverty*) and Goal 8 (*Decent Work and Economic Growth*) of the 2030 Agenda were important to Yunus for his micro-credit projects. Yunus's idea was to fight poverty by opening a bank which lent money to the poorest people but only if they had small businesses. What do you think? Is it good to help someone start a new business? Why? Discuss in class.

HUMAN RIGHTS AND WORKERS' RIGHTS

Rigoberta Menchú Tum

A little big "campesina"

▶ 6 Little Rigoberta Menchú Tum was born in the mountains of Guatemala in a village founded by her parents, who were *campesinos* and grew coffee, cotton and sugar cane*. At only 5 years of age, she began working in the fields with her family. The Indios like her and her family picked coffee on the plantations* on the Pacific coast. They had to work very quickly and very hard, almost like slaves* and some of her brothers and many of her friends even died on the plantations, the *finca*.

Picking coffee.

Rigoberta was very proud of her people and her culture. The Maya from Guatemala had existed for a thousand years and they had had a rich and wonderful history. However, they had disappeared after a short time, because of the arrival of Europeans. It was while she was picking coffee in the silence of the plantation and seeing that her life was only worth a coffee bean that she began to feel the desire to rebel and to defend her right to be a human being worthy of respect.

sugar cane plants that sugar comes from
plantations large areas where plants are grown to be sold
slaves people who are made to work for no money

40

HUMAN RIGHTS AND WORKERS' RIGHTS

The Maya

The history of the ancient Mayan people, one of the largest pre-Columbian civilisations from the area between Yucatan and Guatemala, is well-known. Historians still don't understand how, after such a wonderful period, they could have disappeared so quickly and for no real reason. The mystery of the Maya is even more incredible if we think of their amazing knowledge of astronomy*, arithmetic and also architecture. The Pyramids of the Sun and the Moon are very famous.

Indigenous human rights

At the age of twenty, Rigoberta began to take an active part in the defence of the indigenous community and the organisation of a people's movement. In 1979 she joined a trade union*, the Committee of the Peasant Union (CUC), with her father Vicente. Sadly, in that same year, she lost her brother, father and mother. After these sad events, she spoke out against the government and was sent away from her country. In 1981, Rigoberta escaped to Mexico and decided not to give up her fight. She then travelled all over the world to tell everyone about how the Guatemalan Indios, in particular, were exploited*.

astronomy the study of the universe
trade union organisation which protects workers' rights
exploit to use someone

Rigoberta Menchú Tum

Rigoberta chose to protest in a non-violent way. Non-violent and peaceful protests were a great way for her to fight against political and social injustice. She slowly became a real activist, organising strikes* and trying to persuade indigenous peoples and the *campesinos* that they also had the right to be free. Her battle shows the courage of women fighting for their rights. Rigoberta cannot read or write, but she speaks with so much energy and more and more Guatemalans are joining her fight. Nobody thought that a simple *campesina* could become so important, almost a leader. In the 90s she returned to her country to begin talks with the government.

Words, the only defence

> **"** The world is not going to change unless we change ourselves. **"**

She joined the UN Human Rights Committee as an ambassador and helped to write a declaration on the rights of indigenous peoples. In 1992, at the age of 33, Rigoberta Menchú received the Nobel Peace Prize *"for her struggle for social justice and ethno-cultural reconciliation based on respect for the rights of indigenous peoples"*. When she accepted the prize she said: *"I consider this Prize, not as a reward to me personally, but rather as one of the greatest conquests in the struggle for peace, for Human Rights and for the rights of the indigenous peoples.*

This represents a sign of hope in the struggle of the indigenous people in the entire Continent. It is also a tribute to the Central-American people who are still searching for their stability, for the structuring of their future, and the path for their development and integration, based on civil democracy and mutual respect".

Her battle also included learning to read and write. The Indios usually just spoke to their children about their culture and history because many of them

strikes stopping working to protest against injustice

HUMAN RIGHTS AND WORKERS' RIGHTS

couldn't read or write. Not being able to speak Spanish too, made the Indios weaker and easier to exploit. They didn't know how to write so they signed work contracts with their thumb and ink. The rest of the world knew what was happening to these people and so, for that reason, Rigoberta learnt to speak Spanish, which allowed her to be understood by many more people and to write her autobiography.

> " *I am like a drop of water on a rock. After drip, drip, dripping in the same place, I begin to leave a mark, and I leave my mark in many people's hearts.*". "

My name is Rigoberta Menchú

Her biography, written in 1983 with the historian Elisabeth Burgos, while she was in Mexico, is about the life of a young *campesina*. She describes the situation of the Guatemalan people and, in particular, her own ethnic group, the Quiché. The book describes the traditional customs and beliefs of the Indios of today, which are similar to the ones of the ancient Maya. There are descriptions of indigenous life and their respect for nature. They eat what they grow, their houses are made from plants and the animals are like part of the family. For the Maya, the most important things in life had been sharing, their work, and the community. In poems and books like *The Girl from Chimel*, Rigoberta has written about the important things that her grandfather believed in and the ancient stories he had told her when she was a child.

Rigoberta Menchú Tum

"The only battle you lose ...

... is the one you abandon". With these words Rigoberta shows that, still today, she is an example of freedom and peace in the world. It has always been important for her to keep fighting. Today Rigoberta has meetings all over the world, dressed in traditional Mayan clothes, to tell the story of her people, fight for workers' rights and promote fair and sustainable trade. Guatemala is still the only Latin American country with the greatest number of indigenous peoples. By telling her story, Rigoberta is not just talking about herself. She is the voice of indigenous peoples and their suffering, all over the world. Through her personal experience, she makes us understand that each person's life is worth millions of times more than a coffee bean.

Fair and sustainable trade

"*Fair and sustainable trade*" is a form of business that makes sure the fairest price is paid to a producer and his workers, giving them a profit, not exploiting them and also respecting the land. It respects the rights of workers, gives them self-respect and offers them more opportunities, because they receive payment before the products have been sold.

ACTIVITIES

Reading Comprehension

1 **Which sentences are true (T) or false (F)?**

		T	F
1	At only 5 years of age, she began working in the fields with her family.	☐	☐
2	The Indios are not able to pick coffee because they don't grow it.	☐	☐
3	The Mayan people were one of the largest pre-Columbian civilisations.	☐	☐
4	Rigoberta escaped to Mexico.	☐	☐
5	Rigoberta studied Spanish at school because it was the Guatemalan national language.	☐	☐
6	She joined the UN Human Rights Committee as an ambassador.	☐	☐
7	In Guatemala, there are more women than men, especially in the mountains.	☐	☐
8	Fair and sustainable trade means respecting both workers and the land.	☐	☐
9	Guatemala is the only Latin American country with the greatest number of indigenous people.	☐	☐
10	Rigoberta still lives in Mexico today because she cannot return to her home country.	☐	☐

Speaking The 2030 Agenda - Goal 2

2 **Goal 2 of the 2030 Agenda is *"Zero Hunger"*. In some countries, people are still dying from hunger and thirst. Buying fair trade and sustainable products helps provide food and clean drinking water in rural villages.**
Work in pairs to find out what *"fair trade and sustainability"* means. Which products in our shops should we buy?

Think on!

3 There are some fair trade and sustainable food products which we should look at first, before buying other products, when shopping. Look at the pictures below and decide which ones they are. Discuss the reasons for your choice with the class.

Grammar

4a Join the two sentences together, using the word in brackets.

1. Rigoberta <u>was picking</u> coffee. She understood that not all workers were given the same respect. *(while)*
2. Rigorberta <u>is</u> very proud of her culture. She always dresses in traditional clothes. *(because)*
3. She <u>fights</u> for workers' rights. She is an example to all men and women. *(since)*
4. The Maya <u>disappeared</u> so quickly and for no real reason. They are still seen as mysterious and amazing. *(since)*
5. Rigoberta <u>speaks</u> out against exploitation. She is making things better for the Indios. *(because)*
6. Rigoberta <u>was</u> a simple campesina. Nobody thought that she would become world famous. *(since)*

4b Rewrite the sentences in exercise 4a, using the present participle (verb + ing with no subject) of the verbs <u>underlined</u>. Add 'by' or 'while' before the present participle where needed.

PEACE AND SPIRITUALITY

Thich Nhat Hanh

Engaged Buddhism

▶ 7 Thich Nhat Hahn was born in Vietnam in 1926. When he became a Buddhist monk* at 16 years old, he entered the temple of Tu Hieu, in the city of Hue. As a young man, while he was studying at the University of Saigon, he actively helped to make Buddhism more popular in Vietnam. When the war started in Vietnam, the monks were worried and discussed if they should continue to meditate* or help those who were suffering. Thich chose to do both and founded a sort of *"engaged Buddhism"*. It is the form of Buddhism that supports peace, justice and the fight against global warming.

> *"Meditation is not an evasion; it is a serene encounter with reality. Once there is seeing, there must be acting. With mindfulness, we know how to help and how not."*

Its method always starts with the spirit. The master invites you to look deep into yourself, to try to think of good things and not negative things. Even when he saw the worst things in life, he tried to think about what each of us can do to make this world a better place. Most of all, he wanted everyone to have the opportunity to be a Buddhist, if they wanted to. Through his simple but profound* teachings, the ability to promote peace has reached many more people.

monk religious person who lives in a monastery
meditate stopping to think and look for inner peace
profound deep

PEACE AND SPIRITUALITY

He used his vision of Buddhism in all parts of society: education, economics, technology, the environment. Everything he did every day – walking, eating, washing – had great importance and was a reason for happiness. It's an amazing way to have peace, clarity and understanding, which helps us to have a more active role in the world. Thich was a spiritual leader, as well as the most popular master of Zen in the world.

Buddhism

It is one of the most ancient and most popular religions in the world. It began between the 6th and 5th century BC with the teachings of an Indian monk called Siddhartha, and was founded on Four Noble Truths. Buddhism became a philosophy as well as a religion and is a life education. Its most important values are altruism*, giving no importance to material objects, compassion* and inner peace. Buddhists use these values to live a life that leads to enlightenment, knowing yourself, according to the teachings of Buddha. There are around 400 million followers in the world.

altruism thinking of others before yourself
compassion understanding when people need help and trying to help

The Small Peace Corps

In the early 60s, he taught in some American universities and founded the School of Youth for Social Services, with ten thousand volunteers working in accordance with the Buddhist principles of non-violence and compassion. He also founded a Buddhist university in Saigon, a publishing house and an important pacifist newspaper. He never stopped. He left the United States to go to Europe to promote peace

Thich
Nhat Hanh

and look for a way to end the Vietnam war. During this period in 1966, he met Martin Luther King, who put his name forward as a candidate for the Nobel Peace Prize. *"He is an apostle of peace and non-violence"*, said King.

During the war in Vietnam, he spoke about peace and created the non-violent resistence movement, the Small Peace Corps: groups of lay* people and monks who went into the Vietnamese countryside, going from village to village, to start up schools and hospitals and try to rebuild villages that were destroyed. The Small Peace Corps were not liked by the Vietcongs nor by the Americans, because nobody understood their desire for peace. But they continued to fight for peace and refused to use violence.

As a result of Thich's peace mission, the governments of both North and South Vietnam did not allow him to return to his homeland. So, Thich had to stay away for 39 years! In this period, he continued to travel, carrying his message of peace and brotherhood all over the world. He asked political leaders to end the Vietnam War and also led the Buddhist delegation at the Paris Peace Talks in 1969. When the peace treaty* was signed, he decided to live in France where he taught at the Sorbonne and founded a very famous Buddhist community which still exists.

lay having faith without having a religion
treaty paper signed by countries to agree on something

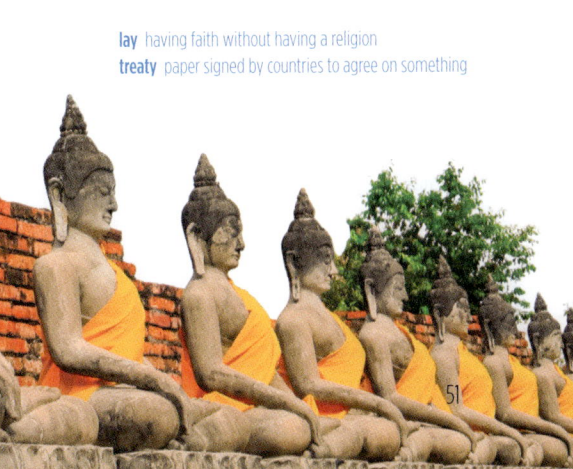

PEACE AND SPIRITUALITY

Plum Village

In 1982, Thich opened Plum Village, a community of monks and lay men and women, near Bordeaux in southwest France. He lived there and taught the art of how to live in peace. As the spiritual leader of this community, he made this the biggest and busiest Buddhist monastery* in the West. More than 200 monks live there and every year they have ten thousand visitors from all over the world.

> *Our own life has to be our message.*

Thich's great idea was to make Buddhism simpler and more in touch with modern day problems. The master, the *thay*, was a peaceful and fearless figure who used movements, smiles and thoughts to teach others the harmony of thought, speech and action within them. His ability to change people's lives was a very special quality. He believed that people could have compassion and love for others, and this made him a perfect master, who was able to bring peace to the world.

Plum Village welcomes people of every age, country and religion and allows them to practise ancient Buddhism: meditation while walking, sitting and eating, deep relaxation and work meditation. It teaches you to stop, smile and be aware of how you are breathing. Every 15 minutes, the whole community stops and takes 3 breaths, just enough time says the master, to open your mind in that moment and feel peace.

monastery place where monks and priests live

Thich **Nhat Hanh**

Wake up!

Thich Nhat Hanh founded Wake Up, an international movement followed by thousands of young people who practise mindfulness and peace. It also has a training programme for teachers called *Wake Up Schools*, to show them how to teach these practices in schools in Europe, America and Asia.

The last goodbye

His last appearance took place in the temple in Tu Hieu, where he had become a Buddhist monk at the age of 16. At the age of 80, when he was ill, he wanted to return to the monastery to live out the rest of his days. Although his illness meant he was unable to speak and also had to use a wheelchair, Thich Nhat Hanh continued to visit the temple altars regularly and teach meditation around the lakes and monuments of the ancestors. His return to the temple reminded everyone how important and special it was to have a deep and truly spiritual life. He died there at midnight on 22nd January 2022 at the age of 95.

ACTIVITIES

Think on!

1 **Here are ten of Thich Nhat Hanh's teachings on life and happiness. Match them to the meanings below (a – j). Which ones do you like the most? Compare your answers with the class and explain why you chose them.**

1. ☐ Value the power of a kind word, a touch or a smile.
2. ☐ If you love someone, the greatest gift you can give them is your presence.
3. ☐ To be beautiful means to be yourself.
4. ☐ Walk as if you are kissing the Earth with your feet.
5. ☐ Because you are alive, everything is possible.
6. ☐ When another person makes you suffer, it is because he suffers deeply within himself.
7. ☐ Blaming others has no positive effect.
8. ☐ Let go of what you don't need and you'll be happy.
9. ☐ In true love you gain freedom.
10. ☐ Life is only in the present moment.

a Every one of us is unique and special.
b If you learn from your mistakes, you can solve everything.
c Move and live slowly, respecting the Earth.
d Small actions are important.
e A man at peace with himself does not want to cause suffering.
f Love isn't possession: real love is freedom.
g You can't return to the past, the future is unknown. Happiness is living well in the present.
h Letting go of unnecessary things is the first step to happiness.
i Always carry the message of peace and love with you.
j Always being present shows great love.

Vocabulary

2a Work in pairs. Write the meanings of these words which you will find in the text about Thich Nhat Hanh.

1 look deep into yourself
2 compassion
3 inner peace
4 meditation
5 harmony
6 deep relaxation

2b Now use each of the above words in exercise 2a in a sentence.

1 ....
2 ....
3 ....
4 ....
5 ....
6 ....

Idioms

3 Match the following idioms to the correct meaning a or b.

1 Be in two minds about something
   a Not able to decide
   b Have lots of ideas
2 Feeling on top of the world
   a Feeling great
   b Feeling like going to the North Pole
3 Light-hearted
   a Very quickly, in a hurry
   b Not worried, happy
4 Have a heart of gold
   a Have health problems
   b Be a very good person

WOMEN AND PEACE

Leymah Gbowee

Making changes

▶ 8 Leymah Gbowee was born in Monrovia, Liberia, in 1972, and was only seventeen when the first civil war began in her country. In Liberia, the people suffered poverty and violence, the children were used as soldiers, and hundreds of thousands of people died. Leymah returned to Liberia, after studying at university in the United States, and had to live through a war which lasted 14 years. It took many friends and family members from her, but also her hopes and dreams. She really wanted to do something to change her country and so she studied to become a social worker*, working in particular with ex-child soldiers. She believed that only women could really change things, so in 1999, when the second civil war started, she really got involved.

social worker someone who helps people in difficulty

Child soldiers

The problem of child soldiers is a humanitarian emergency, an act of violence and one of the most serious violations of children's rights. Hundreds of thousands of boys and girls in at least 14 countries in the world are child soldiers, but official numbers do not exist. They are kept secret because it is prohibited* under international conventions. The International Day against the Use of Child Soldiers (known as Red Hand Day) is 12th February, when the United Nations tries to have ex-child soldiers returned to society to live a normal life again. It is very difficult to do, but it is possible.

prohibited not allowed, not legal

WOMEN AND PEACE

The woman who stopped the war

Leymah decided to get involved personally in humanitarian actions and the fight for peace. Together with Comfort Freeman, the President of a Lutheran Church, she founded and ran WIPNET (the Women in Peacebuilding Network) in Liberia. She spoke direcly to the President of the country at that time, Charles Taylor, and in an open letter she wrote: *"In the past we kept silent, but after seeing our children and our families destroyed by war, it taught us that the future is saying NO to violence and YES to peace"*.

At the Network meeting, women from all of the eighteen West African countries came to share experiences, talk about what the war had taken away from their lives, and learn many things about the war and how to stop it. Leymah thought that no-one else was doing this, that no-one wanted peace, and that only women could really stop the war.

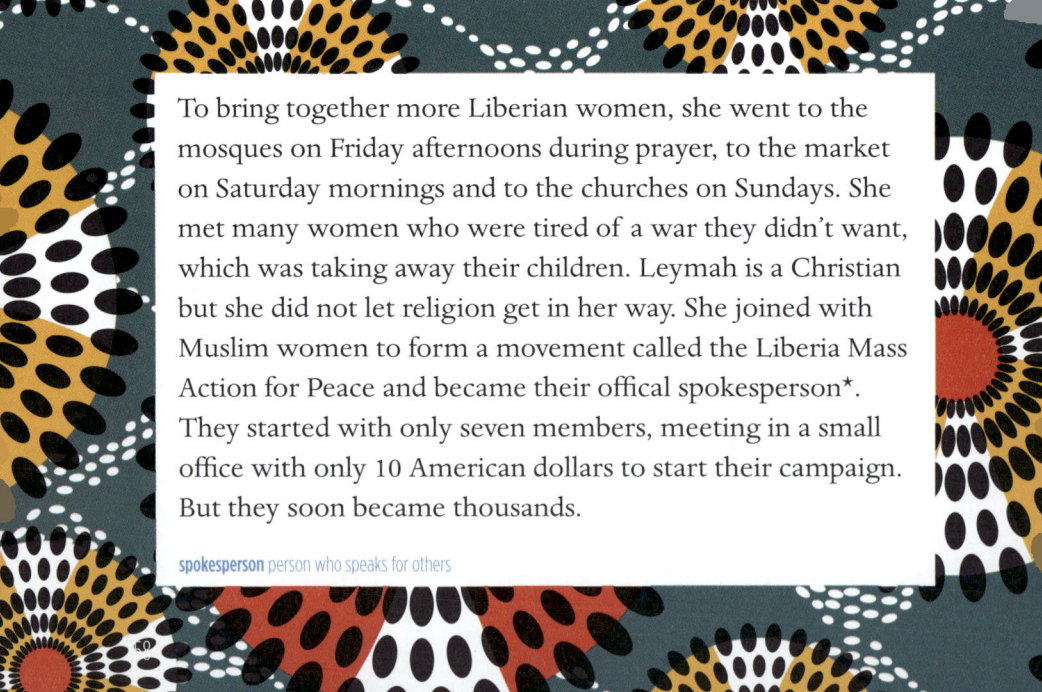

To bring together more Liberian women, she went to the mosques on Friday afternoons during prayer, to the market on Saturday mornings and to the churches on Sundays. She met many women who were tired of a war they didn't want, which was taking away their children. Leymah is a Christian but she did not let religion get in her way. She joined with Muslim women to form a movement called the Liberia Mass Action for Peace and became their offical spokesperson*. They started with only seven members, meeting in a small office with only 10 American dollars to start their campaign. But they soon became thousands.

spokesperson person who speaks for others

Leymah **Gbowee**

> " *We must continue to unite in sisterhood to turn our tears into triumph.* "

In 2003, in the middle of the fighting of the civil war, the activists, dressed in white clothes, organised prayer meetings, sit-ins, demonstrations and strikes and, all in the name of non-violence, they tried to persuade the warlords to make peace. Then they all met in Accra in front of the hotel where they were having peace talks. They wanted to do something important, so they blocked the hotel exit until a peace treaty was reached. *"When women get together, great things happen"*.

The power of women

Leymah received the Nobel Peace Prize in 2011, together with Ellen Johnson Sirleaf, the President of Liberia, and Tawakkul Karman, a Yemeni activist. At the awards ceremony, she gave a beautiful message to the brave women who had fought with her for peace. *"Liberian women, thank you for making our country proud. Thank you for sitting in the rain and under the sun. This is your prize. This is our prize"*.

Leymah united Christian and Muslim women and with them, she started a real revolution for peace. Their non-violent movement succeeded thanks to the hard work of a few brave women, united against war. They wanted to give hope to future generations and protect their children, their land and their future.

Thanks to the work of Leymah and her women, in 2003, the second Liberian civil war ended. After the war, a period of peace began and in 2005, her friend and colleague, Ellen Johnson Sirleaf, won the presidential elections. She was the first woman leader of an African state.

WOMEN AND PEACE

Peace is the only way

In 2012, after receiving the Nobel Prize, Leymah started the Gbowee Peace Foundation Africa in her city of Monrovia, to promote the education and leadership of women, girls, and young people. She now lives in Accra and is the director of the Women in Peace and Security Network. Now all over West Africa, there is a peace programme for women and she has said that *"peace is a process, not an event"*.

Leymah believes that the only way to keep peace is to stop violence, because war is bad for everyone, both winners and losers. Peace is the only way to rebuild a united and civilised society that will last for a long time. Peace is the only thing worth fighting for.

> *"We were aware that the end of the war would come only through non-violence, as we had all seen that the use of violence was taking us and our beloved country deeper into the abyss of pain, death and destruction."*

Leymah **Gbowee**

An army of women

In her book, Mighty Be Our Powers, she writes: "*This is not a war story. It is about an army of women in white, standing up when no one else would - unafraid, because the worst things imaginable had happened. It is about the determination*, clarity and courage we showed, opposing war and bringing peace back to our land. A story you will have never heard because it is the story of an African woman, which is not often told. I want you to hear my story*". The book tells a real, strong and moving story, which starts with desperation* and ends in hope. It does not celebrate the author but tells the very human story of a fragile and weak woman who had so much energy and determination. ◼

determination really wanting to do something   **desperation** having no hope

ACTIVITIES

Reading Comprehension

1 Correct the mistakes in the following sentences.

1 Leymah was only seven when the civil war started in her country.
....

2 Fortunately, the war in Liberia lasted for a short time and many people died.
....

3 The problem of the child soldiers is not a violation of children's rights.
....

4 Leymah wrote a letter to George W. Bush, the American President.
....

5 She believed that only children could stop the war.
....

6 Leymah is a Muslim and goes to the Mosque every Friday to pray.
....

7 To stop the war, Leymah and the women stood in front of the armoured tanks.
....

8 The women who stopped the war were all dressed in red.
....

Vocabulary

2 Leymah Gbowee received the Nobel Peace Prize together with Tawakkul Karman, an activist, journalist and pacifist from Yemen, whose work involved, in particular, women, peace and freedom in the Middle East. She founded "Women Journalists Without Chains"

which defends the freedom of opinion and speech. Tawakkul had to leave her home country and now lives in a city in Turkey.

In the grid below, find and cross out the words from Leymah's story, which you will find horizontally and vertically. Below, write the letters that remain, to make the name of the city that Tawakkul lives in now.

C	H	R	I	S	T	I	A	N
E	M	E	R	G	E	N	C	Y
V	O	W	H	P	C	I	H	S
I	S	H	O	E	A	T	I	A
O	Q	I	P	A	M	W	L	A
L	U	T	E	C	P	O	D	F
E	E	E	S	E	A	M	N	R
N	S	O	L	D	I	E	R	I
C	I	V	I	L	G	N	B	C
E	L	I	F	E	N	U	L	A
T	R	E	A	T	Y	S	U	N

__ __ __ __ __ __ __ __

3 Answer the questions.

1 Why did Leymah Gbowee say that only women could stop the war?
2 Leymah Gbowee believes that "peace is a process, not an event". What do you think that means?
3 The problem of child soldiers is very serious. Why do children become soldiers?
4 Leymah unites women, no matter what their religion is. Do you think that there is strength in numbers? Have you ever felt stronger when you were together with other people?

Speaking

Agenda 2030 - Goal 16

4 Goal 16 is *"Peace, justice and strong institutions"*. Its goal is to *"promote peaceful and inclusive societies, reducing all forms of violence and stopping corruption and the flow of illegal arms and money"*. Imagine you are a politician: persuade your class that our future is peace. Explain what you will do in your country and the rest of the world to reach this important goal. The rest of the class will listen to you carefully and, at the end of your speech, will be allowed to ask you questions. Each person in the class can then take the role of the politician and do the same.

IN DEFENCE OF CHILDREN

Kailash Satyarthi

Searching for the truth

▶ 9 Kailash Satyarthi was born into a middle-class family in India on 11th January 1954. He was an excellent student and graduated in electronic engineering. He was a great admirer of Mahatma Gandhi because of his non-violent fight for freedom and equality, and his ability to show respect also to the weakest people. When he was 11 years old, he discovered that some of his friends had to leave school because their parents didn't have enough money to pay for school books. So, he invented a book bank. With his schoolfriends, he collected old school books and some money to give to the poorest families so that their children could go to school.

"*Anger is power and energy. If we stay within the limits of our egoism, anger changes into hate, violence, vendetta, destruction. But we can break this circle and anger can be changed into ideas and actions. We can go beyond these limits, using our compassion and making the world better. We have to use our anger to do good for all of society. We can use our anger to change the bad things in the world, and that is what I want to do.*"

IN DEFENCE OF CHILDREN

At the age of 15, when India was celebrating the centenary of the birth of Gandhi, he was surprised to hear some Indian leaders speaking against the class system and the discrimination against lower classes, who are referred to as *"untouchable"*. In India, people of the lowest class are not allowed to enter temples, houses or shops belonging to those from a higher class. Kailash was angry about this inequality and wanted to protest against it. He changed his surname, Sharma, which showed which class he belonged to, and became Satyarthi, which means *"one who looks for the truth"*. This anger made him start his fight for peace, and it was this anger that gave him his power and energy.

Saving the children

After leaving university, he taught at a school in Bhopal, but only for a short time. At the age of 26, he left teaching. In 1980, he began his fight against the exploitation of children and fought for the abolition* of child labour* in India. He started the movement Bachpan Bachao Andolan (Save Childhood Movement), the first organisation in India against child labour which helps children who are made to work in factories. Kailash and his colleagues went into factories that make bricks and carpets, where children have to work for many years to earn money to help their parents who have many debts*. Small children, of around six or seven years of age, have to work 14 hours a day, without a break or a day off. It is a sad reality.

abolition using the law to stop something bad
child labour children working illegally
debts money you have to pay back

Kailash
Satyarthi

Child labour

Child labour is an international problem. 152 million children and teenagers, 64 million girls and 88 million boys, are suffering because of child labour. Half of them are doing work which is dangerous for their health, safety and moral development. Child labour takes away their childhood and their self-respect, and is bad for their mental and physical development. Child workers cannot go to school, play or socialise. This means they have no basic human rights.

Over his many years of working to defend children's rights, in 144 countries, Kailash has freed 83,000 children who were working as slaves. That was not enough, however. The children had to be helped to slowly return to a normal life. He opened schools in hundreds of villages where the children could study. Kailash believed that exploitation is the main reason for poverty, unemployment, and children not being able to read and write. Child labour is one of the violations of basic human rights and is not simply a social problem. If poverty comes from ignorance, then it is necessary to fight against child slavery and make sure that every child in every country has an education. The name of his programme is clear. It is called *"Education for All"*.

In 1994, he founded the network *Rugmark*, now called *GoodWeave* International, the first system which checks and certifies that carpets have been made without using child labour. An international campaign was begun to educate people buying these products. Anyone buying a carpet with this certificate can be sure that no children are working in the factory that produced it. It is a great success.

IN DEFENCE OF CHILDREN

Child labour in South Asia has been reduced by 80%. Kailash would also like to do the same in factories that produce sportswear, knitwear* and similar products.

> " Slavery cannot exist in a civilised society. It is intolerable, unacceptable, and not negotiable. "

knitwear clothes made from wool, knitted clothes

The Global March

His work as an activist, thinker and communicator continued with the greatest campaign and biggest non-governmental organisation (NGO), working with children, in the world: the Global March against Child Labour. Since 17th January 1998, the March has reached all corners of the planet, informing the media from all over the world and involving very many people. It fights for the education and social integration of exploited children all over the world. Thanks to Kailash, people march in all the countries of the world for children's rights to a happy childhood.

Kailash Satyarthi

His personal battle for the abolition of child labour has reduced the number of child workers in the world by a third in the last 15 years, and reduced the number of those not going to school by half. Thanks to his work, the Convention against all forms of child labour has been taken on by the International Labour Organization (ILO) and signed by 172 countries. This historical event is something which is, at last, protecting children from the worst sorts of exploitation.

> ❝ *Each time when I free a child, the child who has lost all his hope that he will ever come back to his mother, I see the first smile of freedom. And the mother, who had lost all hope that her son or daughter could ever come back, becomes so emotional and the first tear of joy rolls down her cheek. I see God in it,"* he said. *"This is my biggest inspiration."* ❞

In 2014, when Kailash had already received many international awards and was one of the few civilians to take part in meetings at the General Assembly of the United Nations and the Human Rights Council, he was in his office in New Delhi when he saw on Twitter that he had won the Nobel Peace Prize, together with Malala Yousafzai. At the ceremony, he dedicated the prize to those he had helped all his life: *"to all the children in slavery, suffering because of child labour and trafficking★."* ■

trafficking selling and buying illegally

ACTIVITIES

Grammar

1 Underline the correct relative pronoun in the sentences.

1 When Kailash was 11 years old, he discovered that some of his friends had to leave school because their parents, **who / which** were poor, didn't have enough money to pay for school books, **who / which** were too expensive.

2 During the centenary of the birth of Ghandi, **who / whom** was like a hero to Kailash, he listened to Indian leaders speaking about discrimination against people from the lowest classes, **who / which** are called "untouchable".

3 The same anger **that / whom** young Kailash felt, makes people take action and have new ideas **which / who** are important for all of society.

4 Child labour, **which / whose** Kailash fights against, means that children, **who / whom** are very young, have to work for many hours a day without a break.

5 The children, **who / which** were freed, needed special care, **which / whose** also meant teaching them to read and write.

6 Kailash, **who / whom** had already received many international awards, dedicated his Nobel Peace Prize to the people **which / that** he had helped all of his life, the children.

2 Write sentences about Kailash Satyarthi, using the past simple of the verbs below.

1 give ....
2 teach ....
3 leave ....
4 fight ....
5 win ....

Vocabulary

3 Match the correct meaning of the following words from the text to the definitions below (a–h).

1. ☐ admirer
2. ☐ discrimination
3. ☐ exploitation
4. ☐ abolition
5. ☐ childhood
6. ☐ factory
7. ☐ slavery
8. ☐ compassion

a taking advantage of the weakest people in an illegal and violent way
b period in a person's life when they are very young
c someone who likes a person for the good things they have done
d understanding and being worried about how a person feels when they are suffering
e being against someone because they are a different class, race, religion or age
f using the law to stop something bad that is happening to the weakest people
g condition where a person is owned by another person and has no human rights
h industrial building where something is made, then sold

Speaking

Agenda 2030 - Goal 4

4 Work in pairs. The fourth goal of the Agenda 2030 is "Quality Education". Target 4.5 says: *"By 2030, eliminate gender disparities in education and ensure equal access to all levels of education and vocational training for the vulnerable, including people with disabilities, indigenous peoples and children in vulnerable situations"*.

1. What are the basic rights of every child?
2. How can education help children?
3. What do you think makes a child happy?

FREEDOM OF SPEECH

Maria Ressa

"A short brown girl in a big white world"

▶ 10 Maria Ressa (born Maria Angelita Delfin Aycardo) is a Filipino-American journalist and author. She was born in Manila, in the Philippines, on 2nd October 1963. Ressa's father died when she was one year old. When she was ten, her mother married an Italian-American man called Peter Ressa, who adopted her and so she became Maria Ressa. She had grown up speaking only Filipino, but when her mother and stepfather took her and her sister to live in the Unites States, Maria had to learn to speak English. Talking about her arrival in the US, she said *"I landed in New Jersey, where I could barely speak English, and I had to figure out what a short brown kid was going to do in this big white world"*. She did well at the local public school and learnt to play eight musical instruments. In high school, she was in the theatre group and on the student council. She said her experience in the public schools had taught her that *"you can accomplish anything if you work hard enough"*. She studied at Princeton University, where former US First Lady, Michelle Obama, was her classmate. After leaving university in 1986 with a degree in English, she returned to Manila to study political theatre at the University of the Philippines Diliman, where she also taught journalism.

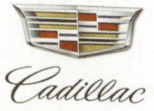

FREEDOM OF SPEECH

Return to her roots*

Her return to the Philippines was at a time of protests and demonstrations by the people in the country, known as the People Power Revolution. As the country moved away from total government control towards democracy, Ressa started a career in journalism. At first, she worked for Philippine government TV stations and then, thanks to her American accent, she got the job of Manila Bureau Chief at CNN in 1988. She was the youngest person ever to be a Bureau Chief at CNN and was the network's main investigative reporter in Asia for 17 years, reporting on major political events in Southeast Asia. In 2005, she returned to the Philippine TV channel ABS-CBN as head of the news division.

Fake* news

After the terrorist attacks in the United States on 11th September 2001, Ressa investigated the growth of terrorist groups in Southeast Asia and how they used social media to communicate and spread information. She knew that social media could bring positive change but she also began thinking about how social media was being used for bad things, as well as good. She believes that authoritarian governments who use disinformation* (fake news), to control the people of their country are a danger to democracy. She also thinks that social media companies have too much power and should control what is being posted on internet.

> **" If you can make people believe lies are the facts, then you can control them "**

---

roots (here) origins
fake false, not true
disinformation giving false facts, fake news

Maria
Ressa

Rappler

In January 2012, with other Filipino journalists, Ressa started an online news website called "*Rappler*", with three main principles – trust*, courage and integrity*. It soon became one of the largest online news sites in the Philippines. She is the Executive Editor and Chief Executive Officer of the news website, which has received many local and international awards. Rappler's goal is to speak the truth and *"build communities of action for a better world"*. However, when they reported on government corruption and human rights violations in the Philippines, the government and the President at that time, Rodrigo Duterte, in particular, did not like what they were writing. Rappler had reported that the Philippine government was using social media to spread disinformation and control people. So, for many years, the government tried to close the website and in 2019, Maria Ressa was arrested and found guilty of libel*. This was seen by human rights groups and journalists as an attack on freedom of the Press.

> " My only crime is to be a journalist, to speak truth to power "

trust believing in someone or something
integrity having this means your are a good, honest person
libel legal word for writing lies about someone

FREEDOM OF SPEECH

Being the good

Maria Ressa has worked for over 35 years as a journalist in Asia, reporting on wars and other dangerous situations. She has seen a lot of bad things but also *"so much good when people, who have nothing, offer you what they have"*. In her fight for freedom of speech and democracy, she has received help from strangers, despite the danger, who want nothing from her personally, but just want to build a better world. She believes that *"to be the good, we have to believe there is good in the world"*.

Ressa has received many awards for her work in journalism and for her courage and work on disinformation, she was named Time Magazine's 2018 Person of the Year. She was among its 100 Most Influential People of 2019, and has also been named one of Time's Most Influential Women of the Century.

In 2021, she received the Nobel Peace Prize, together with the Russian journalist Dmitry Muratov. They were the first journalists since 1935 to have received the Nobel Peace Prize. She won the prize for using freedom of expression to "*expose abuse of power, use of violence and growing authoritarianism in her native country*" and protecting freedom of expression which leads to democracy and lasting peace. In her speech she said, *"Without facts, you can't have truth. Without truth, you can't have trust. Without trust, we have no shared reality, no democracy, and it becomes impossible to deal with our world's existential problems: climate, coronavirus, the battle for truth. What are YOU willing to sacrifice for the truth?"*

Maria **Ressa**

Reporters Without Borders

To many people, Maria Ressa has become a symbol of the fight for press freedom in a country where journalists are in danger. Ressa is one of the 25 leading figures on the Information and Democracy Commission started by Reporters Without Borders. Reporters Without Borders, created in 1992, is an international non-profit and non-governmental organisation with the goal of protecting the right to freedom of information. It also reports the numbers of journalists around the world who have been arrested or killed because of their work in dangerous situations.

The fight goes on

Despite the problems with the Philippine government, Maria Ressa is still trying to keep Rappler going and is continuing her fight for democracy and truth. She lives in the Philippines but, despite legal restrictions, has continued to travel to the United States to visit the universities there and has just published another book called How to Stand Up to a Dictator, which talks about the network of disinformation around the world.

ACTIVITIES

Reading Comprehension

1 Correct the mistakes in the following sentences.

1 Maria Ressa moved to the United States with her mother, step-father and brother when she was ten.
  ....

2 When she arrived in the United States, she was able to speak English very well.
  ....

3 Maria worked for a radio station when she returned to the Philippines.
  ....

4 She believes that *fake news* does not exist and that everything on Internet is true.
  ....

5 Journalists are always safe in all the countries in the world.
  ....

6 Maria now lives in the United States.
  ....

Grammar

2 The following sentences are in Direct Speech. Change them into Reported Speech.

1 When Maria Ressa was 10, she said, "*I can't speak English very well.*"

2 "*I have received a lot of help from strangers*", she said.

3 She said, "*I have seen a lot of bad things*".

4 In her Nobel Peace Prize speech, she said, "*Without facts, you can't have truth and without trust, we have no democracy*".

5 She asked, "*What are you willing to sacrifice for the truth?*"

Vocabulary

3 Read the clues below and complete the crossword.

1. Another name for a journalist
2. The kind of world everybody wants
3. Real facts, not lies
4. The American university that Maria Ressa went to
5. The name of the online news website
6. Another word for bravery
7. When you have to give up something for another thing
8. The continent that Maria Ressa comes from
9. CNN is an American TV news _____
10. Not real, false

Speaking

4 We have all heard about fake news on Internet and social media. How can we know that what we read online is true or false? In pairs, talk about an article or social media post you have seen on Internet and use the questions below to decide if it is true or false and discuss what makes you think this. Compare your answers with your classmates.

- Who wrote this?
- Who do they want to read this?
- Who paid for this? Or, who gets paid if you click on this?
- Who might benefit or be harmed by this message?
- What is missing from this message that might be important?

WORKING TOWARDS A CLEANER WORLD

Ian Kiernan

Building the future

▶ 11 Ian Kiernan (full name Ian Bruce Carrick Kiernan) was born in Sydney, Australia, on 4th October 1940. For the first five years of his life, he didn't see his father very much because he was away from home, fighting in the Second World War. Both his paternal and maternal grandparents were from Scotland. His mother, too, was born in Glasgow, Scotland, and so his parents decided to send him to the Scots College in Sydney when he was seven. When it was time to go to high school, he went to The Armidale School, 500km north of Sydney where he did lots of sports but, most importantly, it was at this time that he discovered his love for sailing*.

When he left high school, he went to the Sydney Technical College where he trained as a builder. After graduating, his father wanted him to come and work with him in his import* business, but Ian was more interested in the building industry. He learnt all about project management and from the 60s to the 80s, he had a very successful business that renovated* houses in the poorest areas of Sydney.

sailing travelling by boat
import to bring things from other countries to sell them
renovated made old building look new again

WORKING TOWARDS A CLEANER WORLD

Sailing to success

During this time, his passion was sailing yachts*. He became a successful professional yachtsman and for more than 40 years, he represented Australia in many sailing competitions around the world. In 1986-1987, he sailed for his country in the BOC Challenge (now known as the Velux 5 Oceans Race), the solo around-the-world yacht race. During this trip, he was sailing in the North Atlantic Ocean when he noticed the large amount of man-made rubbish* in the water and on the shores. Kiernan had already stopped throwing waste* into the ocean while sailing ten years before, because he realised that, although he had learnt to do this from experienced sailors, it was not the right thing to do. But, during this race, when he saw how bad things had become, he was shocked and angry. "*I was shocked, because I knew I had contributed to that rubbish in my earlier behaviour*". He thought that, if he was able to keep his rubbish on board and not throw it into the ocean, surely many others around the world could do the same. "*Each one of us just had to come to the understanding that one person could make a difference.*" Kiernan understood that this rubbish not only came from sailing ships but from people on land too, and that something had to be done to protect the environment and the planet. At the age of 46, Kiernan decided to leave his successful life as a businessman to use his time for much higher goals.

> ❝ *Ordinary people need to lead and not sit there and think that governments are going to spoon-feed* them and look after them and look after the country, because they won't.* ❞

yacht boat with sails
rubbish waste, something you throw away
waste same as rubbish
spoon-feed (metaphor) to give things too easily, like feeding a baby

Clean up

Ian Kiernan

On his return from the BOC race, Kiernan was sailing one weekend with his family near Sydney Harbour, one of the most beautiful harbours in the world. When he saw the broken glass and plastic left on the beaches, he remembered his anger at what he had seen in the ocean during the race, and knew he had to take action immediately. With the help of his friend Kim McKay, he decided to organise a community event to clean up Sydney Harbour. On Sunday 8th January 1989, 40,000 volunteers* came and helped to collect over 5000 tonnes of rubbish. This was only the start of a nationwide campaign to clean up Australia. Since then, more than seven million people in Australia have helped in events throughout the year: *Clean Up Australia* Days, Friday Schools *Clean Up Days* and Business *Clean Ups*. This campaign has made people aware of the need to reduce waste and to limit the use of plastic. People now realise they shouldn't throw rubbish into the rivers and oceans, but also in the countryside and parks.

After the success of the *Clean Up Australia* campaign, Kiernan and McKay founded "*Clean Up the World*" in 1993, with the help of UNEP (the United Nations Environment Programme). By 2007 thirty-five million people from 80 nations had taken part in events in their own countries and in 2017, there were around 120 countries taking part. Now, *"Clean Up the World"* is one of the largest environmental programmes in the world, and unites groups, schools, businesses and local government in over 130 countries to clean up the environment and protect our planet.

volunteer someone who wants to help and works for no money

WORKING TOWARDS A CLEANER WORLD

Plastic Pollution

According to UNEP, plastic pollution increased from two million tonnes in 1950, to 348 million tonnes in 2017 and is expected to double by 2040. At the moment, 85% of all rubbish thrown into the ocean is plastic, and 17 million tonnes of plastic entered the ocean in 2021 alone.

Plastic pollutes our air and our oceans, and is dangerous for humans and wildlife. Recycling* alone is not enough. Too much food packaging* made from plastic is a very big part of the problem too. We really have to use more natural alternatives to plastic.

recycling using rubbish to make new things
packaging paper or plastic around food

Ian Kiernan

A Hero of the Environment

Ian Kiernan always described himself as just an "ordinary Australian" and he was admired by many other "ordinary" people, who were also worried about the environment and their local communities. Kiernan showed others how to do something about the problem and get results. In 1991, the Australian Government gave him the Medal of the Order of Australia for the work he was doing to protect the environment and in 1994, he was awarded a prize for Australian of the Year. In the years that followed, he continued his work to clean up the planet and received many awards for his *Clean Up Australia* and *Clean Up the World* campaigns.

Sadly, Kiernan died on 16th October 2018 in Sydney at the age of 78, after a short illness. Hundreds of people went to his memorial service at the Sydney Opera House. He will be remembered as a kind and generous man, who dedicated his life to his country, the world and the environment. He showed the world that one "ordinary" person can make a difference and that people coming together can make great changes for the better.

> "Simple, easy actions can protect the health of our water resources and help save drinking water supplies. There is not one individual who cannot help to make a difference to the health of the environment."

ACTIVITIES

Reading Comprehension

1 Choose the correct answer.

1 Ian Kiernan's grandparents came from:
   a ☐ England   b ☐ Australia   c ☐ Scotland

2 When he left school, Ian wanted to:
   a ☐ build houses b ☐ work with   c ☐ build yachts
                        his father

3 When he was sailing, he noticed a lot of rubbish in:
   a ☐ the South   b ☐ the Indian   c ☐ the North
       Pacific Ocean   Ocean   Atlantic Ocean

4 The first *Clean Up* event in 1989 was in:
   a ☐ the Atlantic b ☐ Sydney   c ☐ businesses
       Ocean   Harbour   and schools

5 In 1994, Ian Kiernan was "Australian of the Year" because:
   a ☐ he was a successful builder
   b ☐ he had sailed all around the world
   c ☐ he had done a lot of good work to help the environment

Vocabulary

2 Choose a word from the list below and write it next to the correct definition.

> renovate • professional • yachtsman
> • rubbish • packaging • environment •

1 _____: someone who sails a boat
2 _____: something you don't need and throw away
3 _____: the natural world we live in
4 _____: someone who does work or sports for money
5 _____: to rebuild or make new
6 _____: paper or plastic put around food to protect it

Grammar

3 Complete the sentences with one of the following prepositions: to, at, in, on, into.

1. Ian Kiernan was born _____ Sydney _____ October 1940.
2. His parents sent him _____ the Scots College _____ Sydney.
3. Ian didn't want to work _____ his father's business.
4. People shouldn't throw rubbish _____ the ocean or _____ the countryside.
5. Kiernan organised an event to clean up Sydney Harbour _____ his return from the race.
6. *Clean Up The World* is one of the largest environmental programmes _____ the world.
7. _____ the moment, 86% of all rubbish in the ocean is plastic.
8. Kiernan's memorial service was _____ the Sydney Opera House.

Think On!

Agenda 2030 - Goal 14

4 Goal 14 of the 2030 Agenda regarding *"Life Below Water"* is to *"conserve and sustainably use the oceans, seas and marine resources for sustainable development"*. Our ocean, the planet's largest ecosystem, is in danger. By 2025, UNEP wants to prevent and reduce plastic pollution.

What do you think our governments can do to help reach this goal? What can each of us do every day to help reduce the use of plastic? What can we use instead of plastic in our everyday lives?

_____
_____
_____
_____

DOSSIER

Let's not forget

Mohandas Gandhi

Known as Mahatma, meaning "great spirit", Mohandas Gandhi was a politician, a spiritual guide and a lawyer from India. He was born in Porbandar on 2nd October 1869 and was killed in Delhi on 30th January 1948.

He fought to free India from the British Empire, but wanted to do this in a peaceful way, by organising strikes, marches, hunger strikes and other protests. Gandhi defended anyone who was exploited, especially women and the "untouchable" lower classes. He was a vegetarian and right to the end of his life, he used hunger strikes as a form of protest. He was sent to prison more than ten times, but continued to show the world that he was against violence. We will always remember him wearing the *dhoti*, a traditional Indian dress, and travelling all over India, carrying his stick.

Martin Luther King

The pastor Martin Luther King was one of the main leaders of the African American movement for civil rights and against racial discrimination. He was born in Atlanta on 15th January 1929, and was killed in Memphis at the age of 39. He fought all his life for the equality of blacks and whites. In 1963, he organised a big pacifist march in Washington for work and freedom. At the end of this march, he made his very famous speech, called "I have a dream", which was shown live on television. He talked about his hopes for a united America that respected the rights of every person. King was a great speaker and he made this speech in front of the Lincoln Memorial, a symbol of the end of slavery. Thanks to his non-violent protests, laws were made that abolished the most serious racial discrimination. He received the Nobel Peace Prize in 1964.

CHANGING THE WORLD!

Tenzin Gyatso

Tenzin Gyatso is a Buddhist monk, born in Tibet on 6th July 1935, who is the fourteenth Dalai Lama. This title means "ocean of wisdom" and refers to a great Buddhist master, spiritual leader and also Tibetan political leader. When he was 15, Tibet was invaded and he had to escape to India. Since then, he has decided to dedicate his life to solving the problems in Tibet in a non-violent way. He has travelled all over the world, speaking to other countries and the United Nations about his non-violent fight for his country. His plan is for Tibet, which is high in the mountains to the north of the Himalayas, to become a peace zone, independent from China, with respect for the culture and basic rights of the Tibetans and their country. He won the Nobel Peace Prize in 1989.

Mother Teresa of Calcutta

Mother Teresa, an Albanian Roman Catholic nun, was born in Skopje on 26th August 1910 and died in Calcutta on 5th September 1997. She founded the Missionaries of Charity and became famous all over the world for her work with poor people in Calcutta and India. She started many missions and always stayed with people who were suffering the most. She received the Nobel Peace Prize in 1979 for her work with very poor people and for the respect she gave to every single person. People all over the world were very sad when she died. In 2003, Pope John Paul II made her "blessed" and then in 2016, Pope Francis declared her a "saint". On her tomb in Calcutta, there is written a phrase from the Gospel, which symbolises her life as a woman of peace: "*Love one another as I have loved you*".

DOSSIER
Peacekeeping Organisations

The UN

The UN (United Nations) was founded in 1945, after the Second World War, with the goal of keeping peace, security and good relations between the 51 member states, on an international level. Its idea was also to promote economic and social develpment and make sure that human rights were always respected. Today the UN has 193 member states and is the only organisation that involves all the countries coming together to solve many world problems, through participation, discussion and the opportunity to make new rules.

Unesco

Unesco (The United Nations Educational, Scientific and Cultural Organization) is an international organisation which protects and promotes artistic and cultural heritage of all types, all over the world. It promotes tourism and economic projects that defend human rights and prevent wars. It was founded in 1945, after the Second World War and now has 200 member states. Together with the UN, it keeps peace and continues dialogue between different cultures around the world and protects historical, cultural and natural sites which they call Unesco World Heritage Sites. Italy is the country with the greatest number of Unesco sites.

FAO

FAO, the Food and Agriculture Organisation is the United Nations agency which fights against world famine. Its motto in Latin is Fiat panis, which means "Let there be bread" and its headquarters is in Rome, Italy. Its work involves agriculture and food production, especially in developing countries. Its goal is to promote better farming and fight against various natural disasters. Even now, there are 3 billion people in the world who have no access to healthy food. So, every year, FAO celebrates World Food Day on 16th October, to remind everyone how important it is that every person in the world has the right to eat well.

CHANGING THE WORLD!

Unicef

Unicef is the UN agency which promotes the rights of children all over the world and improves their living conditions. It works inside 156 developing countries and has programmes in 36 Western countries to collect money for educational projects and to protect children's rights. Unicef is the largest children's international organisation and thanks to its work around the world every year, hundreds of millions of children are protected and receive treatment, vaccines, good food, clean water and a basic education.

WFTO

The World Fair Trade Organisation is a network of around 400 world organisations working to improve the living conditions of the poorest traders, especially those who promote fair and sustainable trade. It was founded in 1989 to help people with businesses, by setting general standards and rules that the workers in fair and sustainable trade have to follow to make sure everyone is treated equally and with respect.

DOSSIER

Important words

Mother Teresa of Calcutta

"If you want a message of peace and love to be heard, it has to be sent out. To keep a lamp burning, we have to keep putting oil in it."

"Not all of us can do great things. But we can do small things with great love, and that is what counts."

"What can you do to promote world peace? Go home and love your family."

Mohandas Gandhi

"Be the change you want to see in the world."

"The path of true non-violence requires much more courage than violence."

"What I have done will endure, not what I have said and written."

CHANGING THE
WORLD!

Martin Luther King

" Injustice anywhere is a threat to justice everywhere. "

" Darkness cannot drive out darkness, only light can do that. Hate cannot drive out hate, only love can do that. "

" Our lives begin to end the day we become silent about things that matter. "

Tenzin Gyatso

" There are only two days in the year that nothing can be done. One is called yesterday and the other is called tomorrow, so today is the right day to love, believe, do and mostly live. "

" Compassion, altruism and a good heart are not only noble sentiments towards others. They also benefit ourselves "

" Give the ones you love wings to fly, roots to come back and reasons to stay. "

FINAL TEST

Decide if the following sentences are true (T) or false (F).

		T	F
1	Malala Yousafzai worked in secret for the Taliban.	☐	☐
2	Malala made a speech at the UN when she was 16.	☐	☐
3	Women in Pakistan aren't as free as men are.	☐	☐
4	Nelson Mandela was a lawyer who defended black people.	☐	☐
5	When Mandela was in prison, he stopped fighting for equality and died.	☐	☐
6	Apartheid was abolished at the end of the Second World War.	☐	☐
7	Wangari Maathai is world famous for being "*the Tree Woman*".	☐	☐
8	Wangari saw the damage to the environment and its effect on the people who needed the plants to live.	☐	☐
9	Biodiversity is an experiment done in a laboratory.	☐	☐
10	Microcredit is used to make banks richer.	☐	☐
11	Professor Yunus founded the "village bank".	☐	☐
12	Rigoberta Menchú Tum's family didn't like what she was doing.	☐	☐
13	Rigoberta was a *campesina*, so she didn't learn to read and write but had to work in the fields.	☐	☐
14	When the war started in Vietnam, Thich Nhat Hahn decided to go away to meditate.	☐	☐
15	Plum Village is a tourist village in Tibet.	☐	☐
16	Leymah Gbowee had to fight in the civil war in Liberia.	☐	☐
17	Leymah united Christian and Muslim women and started a real revolution for peace.	☐	☐
18	Kailash Satyarthi strongly believed in the tradional Indian class system.	☐	☐
19	Kailash knew that children had to be really free from exploitation to have an education.	☐	☐
20	The problem of child soldiers no longer exists.	☐	☐
21	Rappler is a website with gossip from all over America.	☐	☐
22	Maria Ressa says everything you read on Internet is true.	☐	☐
23	Millions of people take part in events for the *Clean Up The World* campaign every year.	☐	☐
24	Ian Kiernan gave up his business to organise events to clean up the environment.	☐	☐

SYLLABUS B1

Level B1

This reader contains the items listed below as well as those included in Levels A1 and A2

Verbs
Present Simple and Continuous
Past Simple and Continuous
Present Perfect Simple
Past Perfect Simple
Future with 'will'

Verb Forms and Patterns
Verbs followed by infinitive
Verbs followed by gerund
Common phrasal verbs with prepositions
Second Conditional
Passive forms: Present and Past Simple
Reported Speech: statements and questions
Modals: could, have to

Subordinate Clauses with when, while, although, since

Time Expressions

Prepositions of Time and Place: to, at, in, on, into

Relative Pronouns

YOUNG ADULT READERS

STAGE 1
Sir Arthur Conan Doyle, *A Study in Scarlet*
Jonathan Swift, *Gulliver's Travels*
Sir Arthur Conan Doyle, *The Hound of the Baskervilles*
Daniel Defoe, *Robinson Crusoe*

STAGE 2
William Shakespeare, *Hamlet Prince of Denmark*
Charles Dickens, *Great Expectations*
William Shakespeare, *Romeo and Juliet*
Bram Stoker, *Dracula*
William Shakespeare, *A Midsummer Night's Dream*
Robert Louis Stevenson, *The Strange Case of Dr Jekyll and Mr Hyde*
Jerome K. Jerome, *Three Men in a Boat*
John Buchan, *Thirty-Nine Steps*
Pauline Russo, *Changing the World!*

STAGE 3
Charlotte Brontë, *Jane Eyre*
Jane Austen, *Pride and Prejudice*
Oscar Wilde, *The Picture of Dorian Gray*
William Shakespeare, *Macbeth*
Jane Austen, *Sense and Sensibility*
Edith Wharton, *The Age of Innocence*
Charles Dickens, *A Christmas Carol*
Wilkie Collins, *The Woman in White*
Anonymous, *Beowulf*
Robert Louis Stevenson, *Kidnapped*
Elizabeth Ferretti, *The Earthkeepers*
Thomas Hardy, *Tess of the d'Ubervilles*
George Orwell, *1984*

STAGE 4
James Joyce, *Dubliners*
Mary Shelley, *Frankenstein*
Henry James, *The Turn of the Screw*
Emily Brontë, *Wuthering Heights*
Edgar Allan Poe, *Stories of Mystery and Suspense*
Charles and Mary Lamb, *Tales from Shakespeare*
Charles Dickens, *A Tale of Two Cities*
Hermann Melville, *Moby Dick*
Jane Austen, *Emma*
Nathaniel Hawthorne, *The Scarlet Letter*
E.M. Forster, *A Passage to India*

STAGE 5
Virginia Woolf, *Mrs Dalloway*
Francis Scott Fitzgerald, *The Great Gatsby*

STAGE 6
Joseph Conrad, *Heart of Darkness*
J. Borsbey & R. Swan, Editors, *A Collection of First World War Poetry*
Oscar Wilde, *The Importance of Being Earnest*